SPACE

First published in Canada by Whitecap Books
351 Lynn Avenue, North Vancouver, British Columbia, V7J 2C4

Text and illustration copyright © Random House Australia Pty
Ltd, 2000

ISBN 1-55285-128-1

Children's Publisher: Linsay Knight
Series Editor: Marie-Louise Taylor
Managing Editor: Marie-Louise Taylor
Art Director: Carolyn Hewitson
Design concept: Stan Lamond
Production Manager: Linda Watchorn

Illustrator: Spike Wademan
Consultant: Dr Paul Payne
Writer: Dr Paul Payne
Educational Consultant: Pamela Hook

Film separation by Pica Colour Separation Overseas Pte Ltd,
Singapore
Printed in Hong Kong by Sing Cheong Printing Co. Ltd.

For permission to reproduce any of the illustrations in this book,
please contact Children's Publishing at Random House Australia,
20 Alfred Street, Milsons Point. NSW 2061. fax: 612 9955 3381

When you see a word in **bold** type, you'll find its
meaning in the Glossary at the back of the book.

SPACE

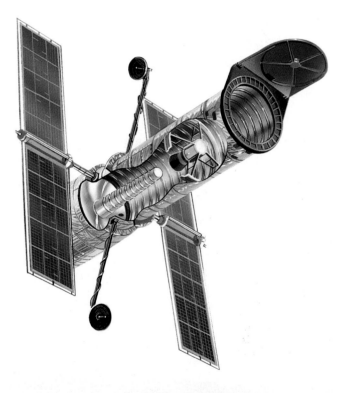

Consultant **Dr Paul Payne**
Illustrator **Spike Wademan**

WHITECAP
B O O K S

CONTENTS

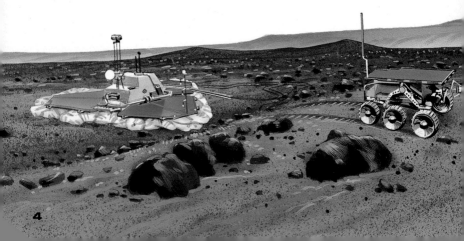

CONTENTS

Looking into space

Look up at the night sky. It is full of thousands and thousands of stars. These stars have been there all your life and will be the same when you are very old.

EARLY OBSERVERS

People have watched the same stars for thousands of years. They studied and named them, they even made patterns from them. These early observers began the study of the sky, called astronomy. Once upon a time astronomers thought the stars had magical powers. We now know this is not true, and that the stars are just like our Sun but very, very far away.

EXPLORING SPACE

Astronomy is the study of everything out in space. Astronomers use telescopes to make everything in space appear closer and brighter. They also build spacecraft to go out and explore the planets and the Sun. Sometimes people also go out into space to see what is there. However we have not gone very far. The Moon is the furthest anyone has ever been. It is the closest thing in space for us to visit. We have a lot more to see and find out. So let us explore space with this book. We will begin our exploration with the Sun and the planets.

LOOK AGAIN!
If you were on the Moon you could see the Sun and stars at the same time.

Buzz Aldrin and Neil Armstrong on the Moon in July 1969.

The Solar System

The Sun is in the centre of our Solar System. Within the Solar System are planets, moons, asteroids and comets. They all move about the Sun on paths called **orbits**. *Our Earth is one of nine planets that* **orbit** *about the Sun. It takes one year for us to go once around the Sun. As we orbit the Sun we take our Moon with us. Many of the other planets also have moons which orbit about them.*

Pluto

Uranus

asteroids

Mars

Earth

Venus

Mercury

Sun

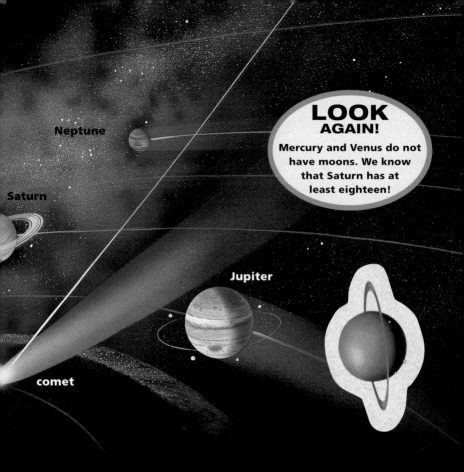

Neptune

Saturn

**LOOK
AGAIN!**

Mercury and Venus do not
have moons. We know
that Saturn has at
least eighteen!

Jupiter

comet

THE PLANETS

All the planets are round and are spinning around. While spinning,
they orbit the Sun. Mercury takes 88 days to go around the Sun,
making it the fastest of all the planets. Pluto is the slowest planet
and takes 248 years. The Sun gives Earth, and all the planets, light
and heat energy. The planets near the Sun are much hotter than
Earth. The planets farther from the Sun are much, much colder.
You can find Mercury, Venus, Mars, Jupiter and Saturn in the night
sky. They look like bright stars. However they do not make light
like the stars. We can see them because they reflect the light of the
Sun. To see Uranus, Neptune and Pluto you need a telescope
because they are so far away.

The Sun

*The Sun is a huge ball of hot hydrogen **gas**. Over 109 Earths could fit across the Sun. On its surface it is 6,000°C (10,832°F)! That is at least ten times hotter than the oven in your kitchen!*

ERUPTIONS ON THE SUN

The surface of the Sun is called the photosphere. The gas here is continually **erupting**. Some of the gas is thrown out into space, which makes a wind blowing away from the Sun. We call this the **solar wind**. Sometimes very violent explosions, called flares, appear near darker spots on the surface. These spots are called sunspots. Each one can be many times bigger than Earth.

Through special telescopes, large streaming arcs of red gas called prominences can sometimes be seen rising from sunspots.

Sunspots are cooler spots on the Sun. Inside a sunspot it is 3,000°C (5,432°F).

Earth is drawn to show its size.

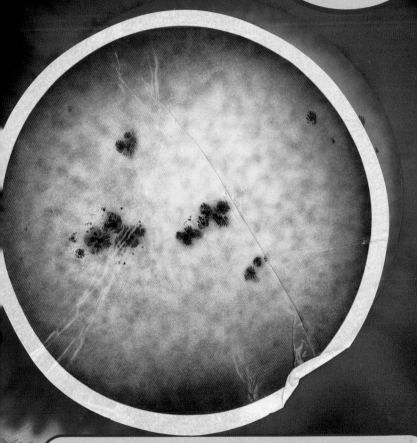

Imagine this picture is the Sun. Let us call it the Model Sun. If the Sun were this big, Earth would be 1 millimetre (1/25 inch) across and orbit 11 metres (36 feet) away. How far from the Sun would all the other planets be? You'll find out as you read through this book. (Use the sticker of our Model Sun on the stickers pages.)

Earth

Earth is a very special planet. It is the only planet we know of that has life. We can breathe the air and drink the water. There are also plants and animals for us to eat, and for most of the time the temperature is just right.

THE BLUE WORLD

From space, Earth looks like a blue world covered with white clouds. Water seems to be everywhere—in the oceans, the clouds, and the frozen ice caps of the North and South Pole. The brown land only covers a third of the planet. We think that water is essential for life to exist. Nothing would be alive on Earth if there was no water. When searching for life on another planet we look for water first. However, it is not the only thing we need. Our **atmosphere** surrounds us and gives us the air we breathe. It also keeps us warm at night. Without the atmosphere we would freeze at night as soon as the Sun set at the end of a day. Of all the planets, Earth is the perfect place for us to live.

In our imaginary solar system, Earth is 11 metres (36 feet) from our Model Sun (see page 11). Place the Model Sun 11 metres (36 feet) away and see how big it appears.

Day and night

Earth is always on the move. Earth spins around like a big ball once in a **day**, and orbits the Sun once in a **year**. One side of Earth is lit by the Sun and everyone there is having day. While the side facing away is in darkness and everyone there is experiencing night. As Earth spins during the day, we see the Sun rise in the east and move across the sky to eventually set in the west. When the Sun disappears the sky is dark and the stars appear for us to see.

Imagine you are now halfway through the night. There is no Sun in the sky and it is very dark. It would be near midnight.

N

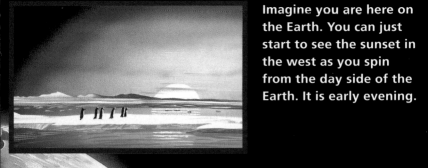

Imagine you are here on the Earth. You can just start to see the sunset in the west as you spin from the day side of the Earth. It is early evening.

Imagine you are here. The Sun would be high in the sky and it would be almost halfway through a day. It would be near midday.

NIGHT FOLLOWS DAY

When we have night, people on the other side of the world have daylight. When you are in bed they are playing in the sunshine. When you wake up they are going to sleep. Imagine you are on the Earth pictured here. What time of day would it be in each of the scenes?

Meteors and asteroids

Look at the sky at night and you will probably see sudden flashes of light and think a star is streaking across the sky and falling to the ground. These flashes are not stars at all, but tiny rocks racing into our atmosphere and burning up.

Maybe the dinosaurs died 65 million years ago when a large asteroid hit Earth.

VISITORS FROM SPACE

These flashes of light in the night are called **meteors**. They can be travelling 300 times faster than a bullet. As they rush into our atmosphere they become very hot as they rub against the air. Just like when you rub your hands together and they become warm. The rubbing of the meteor against the air makes them so hot they glow. Most meteors burn up very quickly. These are about the size of a pea. Sometimes larger meteors enter our night sky.

ACTUAL-SIZE
METEOR

ACTUAL-SIZE
PEA

Larger meteors will be
very bright and may
survive the trip through
the atmosphere to land
on the ground. Meteors
that land on the ground
are called **meteorites**.

COLLISIONS WITH ASTEROIDS

About once every 30 million years a very large rock enters our
atmosphere. It may be as big as a kilometre (about half a mile)
across. We call these rocks asteroids. There are many thousands of
asteroids out in space. Most of them orbit the Sun between Mars
and Jupiter. However some of them come close to Earth. If they
hit Earth a very large hole is made in the ground called a **crater**.
These craters may be as big as 50 kilometres (31 miles) across!

The Moon

The Moon is the nearest object in space to us. Thousands of years ago people thought of a way to measure the distance to the Moon. They found that it is the same distance as 30 Earths placed side by side. They also measured how long it appeared to take the Moon to orbit Earth. This length of time we now call a month, which is approximately 30 days.

OUR LIFELESS MOON

Today we know the Moon is a lifeless place. There is no air or liquid water. It is pitted with many craters that formed 3 billion years ago when large asteroids hit the surface. During all that time the craters have remained almost the same. On Earth, air and water have **eroded** old craters. **Astronauts** have been to the Moon. On the Moon they weighed six times less because the **gravity** is weaker there. You could throw a stone six times higher on the Moon. The astronauts brought back many rocks. These rocks are very similar to ones you might find near a volcano on Earth. One day it is likely that people will build cities on the Moon. In these cities all the people, plants and animals would live inside homes that have their own air and water. We could then mine the Moon for special metals like iron and gold.

The large dark patches on the moon are called mare. People long ago thought they were oceans. We now know they are large flat, dusty plains.

This is the side of the
Moon we can see at night.
We never get to see the
other side.

EARTH   MOON

You can fit 30 Earths in the distance from Earth to the Moon.

Phases of the Moon

The Moon appears to change shape as it orbits Earth. Sometimes it appears as a thin curve and sometimes it is bright round disc. The different shapes of the Moon are called its phases. Why do you think the Moon has phases?

THE SUNLIT MOON

Look at the main illustration, you can see the Moon in different positions around Earth during one orbit. The Moon has a day and night side, just like Earth. From Earth we see different amounts of the bright side as it orbits.

7

8

1

2

Sometimes when it is a new moon the Moon will cover the Sun. This is called a solar eclipse.

VIEWS OF THE MOON

1

Look at the illustrations on the right. They show the Moon as seen from Earth during one month. When the Moon appears to be in nearly the same direction as the Sun we can only see the dark side. The Moon is said to be a New Moon and we cannot see it at all (1). Half a month later, when it has gone through half an orbit, we can see all the day side of the Moon. We call this a full moon (5). In between the new moon and full moon we can see half of the Moon. These are called first quarter (3) and last quarter (7).

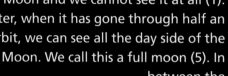
2

3

6

5

4

4

3

LOOK AGAIN!

Why do you think you can sometimes see the Moon in the sky during the day?

5

6

7

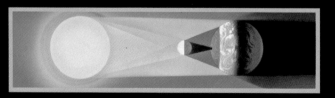

8

Sometimes when it is a full moon the Moon will move into the shadow of Earth. This is called a lunar eclipse.

The International Space Station

The International Space Station is a huge laboratory being built in space. It orbits Earth 360 kilometres (224 miles) above the ground. Many countries are working together on this project. Scientists will live and work onboard the station for many months.

LOOK AGAIN!

In an emergency, astronauts can escape in the small space shuttle, *X33*.

The International Space Station is the biggest structure ever built in space. When it is completed in 2004, it will have as much room inside as the passengers do on a 747 jumbo jet.

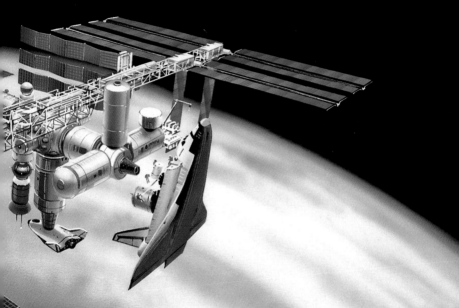

LIVING IN SPACE

People will fly to the station and return to Earth in the space shuttle. People who work in space are called astronauts. One very important experiment that the astronauts will make is to see how long they can be happy and healthy in space. We know that people need gravity to be healthy. Inside the Space Station everything, including the astronauts, has no weight. Everything floats and so there is no gravity. If astronauts are floating for many months they become weak and must return to Earth. We need to find ways of keeping astronauts healthy in space if we are to make the 6 month trip to Mars in the future.

Hot planets

Mercury and Venus are the hottest planets in the Solar System. This is because they orbit so close to the Sun.

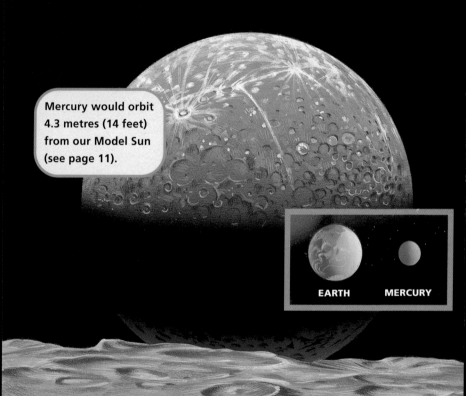

Mercury would orbit 4.3 metres (14 feet) from our Model Sun (see page 11).

EARTH   MERCURY

MERCURY

Mercury is the closest planet to the Sun. It is much less than half the size of Earth and looks very similar to our Moon. Like our Moon, it has many craters. It also does not have any air or water. Because Mercury is so close to the Sun, it is very hot. Standing in the sunlight it is 410°C (770°F). The planet races around the Sun in 88 days, and one day on Mercury is equal to 176 days. Its day is twice as long as its year!

VENUS

Venus is the next planet from the Sun. It has a year of 225 days. It is about the same size as Earth and has a very thick carbon dioxide atmosphere. The carbon dioxide traps the heat from the Sun and makes it very hot. On the surface Venus is 470°C (878°F). This is hotter than Mercury. It is twice the temperature of your oven. In our night sky Venus appears like a very bright star just after sunset or just before sunrise.

EARTH   VENUS

Venus would orbit 8 metres (26 feet) from our Model Sun (see page 11).

Exploring Mars

Mars is known as the red planet. It glows like a red star in the night sky. It is only half the size of Earth. Astronomers think life may have started on Mars a long time ago.

A CLOSER LOOK

Information beamed back from spacecraft has revealed Mars to be a very dry place. The land on Mars looks like a rocky desert on Earth, though Mars is very cold. The hottest place on Mars is like standing on the South Pole of Earth. All the water on Mars has frozen into ice. Mars has a very thin atmosphere, but long ago it was thicker and warmer. Oceans and rivers flowed across its surface. In the water there may have been some form of life.

Mars would orbit 13 metres (43 feet) from our Model Sun (see page 11).

Astronomers have been looking for life on Mars for over a hundred years. Many spacecraft have gone to Mars, and many more will be sent exploring to find life.

In 1877, Giovanni Schiaparelli saw Mars through his telescope. He thought he saw lines on Mars. People later thought these may have been made by aliens. We now know the lines were never there.

SCHIAPARELLI'S MAP

The planet Mars with the large valley, Valles Marineris.

EARTH   **MARS**

The length of a Martian day is about the same as a day on Earth. A Martian year is 687 Earth days long.

Mars 2001

Two spacecraft sent to Mars in 2001 are to study the environment of this planet. They will tell scientists what dangers await people when they go there in the future.

SPACECRAFT EXPLORERS

One spacecraft is called the Orbiter. This spacecraft will orbit Mars and study its surface in great detail. Another spacecraft called the Lander will land on the surface and send out a little rover to explore the Martian ground. We know of many dangers on the surface of Mars but the Lander is designed to look for many more. It will study the dusty surface to see if the fine dust is a hazard to people.

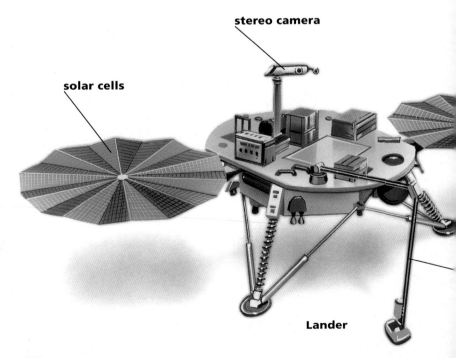

stereo camera

solar cells

Lander

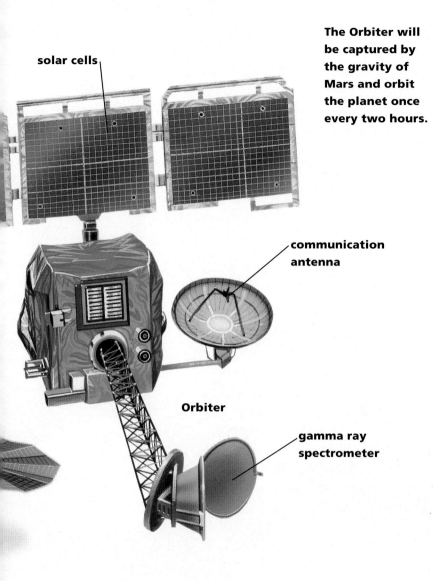

solar cells

The Orbiter will be captured by the gravity of Mars and orbit the planet once every two hours.

communication antenna

Orbiter

gamma ray spectrometer

robotic arm

The Lander will communicate by a radio transmitter to the Orbiter which will then relay the information to Earth.

Jupiter

Jupiter is the largest of all the planets in the Solar System. Over 1,400 Earths could fit inside it. However, it weighs only as much as 314 Earths. This means that it is not as heavy as rock. It is a liquid planet with a thick atmosphere. In our night sky it appears like a very bright white star.

COLD WORLDS

Jupiter is made of the same stuff as stars—**hydrogen** and **helium**. It is very cold because it is five times further from the Sun than Earth. The temperature on Jupiter is about 150°C (-238°F) below zero. The clouds in the atmosphere of Jupiter get stretched around the planet because Jupiter spins very fast. A day on this giant planet is only 10 hours long, but it takes 12 years to orbit the Sun. Astronomers have found a small rocky ring and sixteen moons circling Jupiter. Four of the moons are much larger than the rest. They are called Io, Europa, Ganymede and Callisto. On Io, there is always a volcano erupting. Europa, Ganymede and Callisto are made of rock covered in thick ice.

LOOK AGAIN!

In the middle of Jupiter is core made of rock. This core is about the size of Earth.

JUPITER

EARTH

You could fit eleven Earths across Jupiter.

In the future a spacecraft may explore an ocean under the icy surface of Europa.

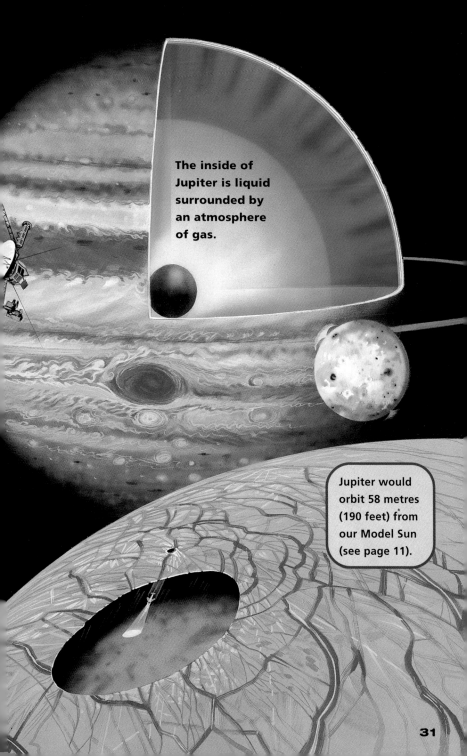

The inside of
Jupiter is liquid
surrounded by
an atmosphere
of gas.

Jupiter would
orbit 58 metres
(190 feet) from
our Model Sun
(see page 11).

Saturn

Saturn is a beautiful planet. It appears at night like a bright yellow star. Through a telescope Saturn is a wonderful sight. It is surrounded by a wide icy ring. When you see Saturn through a telescope you will never forget it.

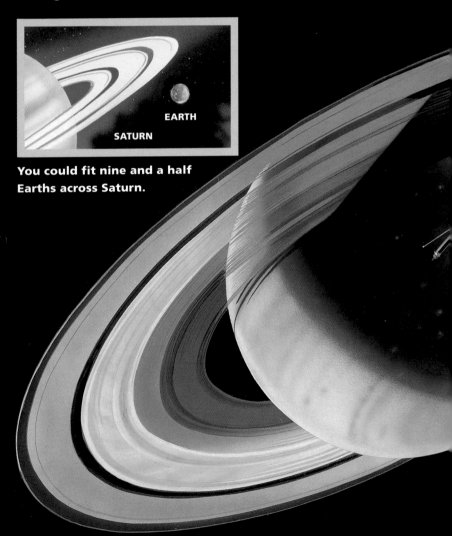

EARTH

SATURN

You could fit nine and a half Earths across Saturn.

Saturn would
orbit 106 metres
(348 feet) away
from our Model
Sun (see page 11).

AN ICY RING

The planet Saturn is very much like Jupiter. It is a liquid
and gas planet, but it is smaller than Jupiter. The rings are
billions of boulders of ice all orbiting the planet. Outside the
rings Saturn has eighteen moons. The largest of these moons is
called Titan. It is the only moon in the Solar System that has a
thick atmosphere. In some ways it is like the atmosphere of Earth,
so maybe there is simple life on Titan. A spacecraft called *Cassini*
will visit Saturn. It will send a probe into Titan's atmosphere to
see what is there.

Cold planets

Uranus, Neptune and Pluto are the most distant planets in the Solar System. They cannot be seen at night with your eyes. You need a telescope to make them appear brighter and closer.

BIG BLUE WORLDS

Uranus and Neptune are big blue worlds. Like Jupiter and Saturn, they are made of liquid and gas. They are both slightly less than half the size of Saturn and both have a small, dark, icy ring system around them. Uranus spins around once in 18 hours while Neptune takes 19 hours to spin around.

Uranus is very unusual because it is tipped over on its side. Maybe in the past a large object hit Uranus and made it fall over.

Uranus would orbit 213 metres (699 feet) Model Sun, and Neptune would orbit 334 (1,096 feet) away; Pluto's orbit would var 329 metres (1,079 feet) to 548 metres (1,7 from our Model Sun (see page 11).

PLUTO

ODD ONE OUT

Pluto is the oddest planet in the Solar System. It is much smaller than any of the other planets and its orbit around the Sun is different to all the other planets. Pluto's orbit is like an oval while the other planets have orbits more like a circle. The orbit is tilted so that Pluto rises up through the Solar System and falls back down again during the 248 years it takes to go around the Sun. Maybe in the future astronomers will decide that Pluto is not a planet after all. It might be one of many icy worlds out past Neptune called **Kuiper objects**.

Pluto has a small moon called Charon. In the future, *Pluto Express* will visit these worlds.

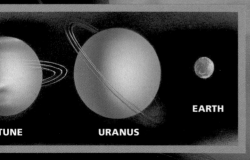

EARTH

TUNE   **URANUS**

The icy boulder in a comet is called the nucleus. For a big comet it may be 15 kilometres (9 miles) across.

The spacecraft *Stardust* collects the dust from the comet nucleus and returns it to Earth.

Comets

Sometimes in the night sky you will see a comet. You may have to wait many years, but it is wonderful to see a big bright comet. A comet looks like a large star with a misty tail. It may appear in the sky for many weeks before fading away.

ICEBERGS IN SPACE

Comets are big boulders of ice floating in space a long way past Pluto. Sometimes one will fall towards the Sun. The heat from the Sun makes some of the ice turn into steam. The solar wind blows back the steam to make a tail. A comet's tail can be many millions of kilometres long. It is then we see the comet in our sky. Astronomers cannot predict many comets so they will appear unexpectedly.

The person who discovers a new comet is allowed to name it. If you find a comet you can call it whatever you like.

LOOK AGAIN!

The shields at the front of *Stardust* protect it from dust within the tail of the comet.

Comets often have two tails—a blue tail made of gas and a brown tail made of very, very small rocks, just like powder. Astronomers call this dust

Stars

We can see thousands of stars shining in the night sky. Many stars are just like our Sun and shine with a yellow light. However, many are also different. Some stars are blue and some red, some are much smaller than our Sun and some are much, much bigger.

COLOURS OF STARS

Stars are very big balls of hydrogen and helium gas. The hydrogen in the centre of stars continually explodes, which creates all the light we see shining from stars. The bigger a young star, the brighter and hotter it will be. It may surprise you to know that the hottest stars are blue and the cooler ones are red. Try to see the colours of the stars at night. If you look carefully you will see many blue stars and only a few red ones. The red stars are dying. They are called red giants. When a star grows old it begins to expand and cool. As the star cools it turns red.

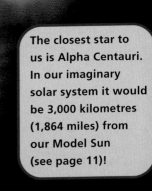

The closest star to us is Alpha Centauri. In our imaginary solar system it would be 3,000 kilometres (1,864 miles) from our Model Sun (see page 11)!

When our Sun becomes a red giant, in 4 billion years, it will be bigger than the orbit of Earth about the Sun!

HOW HOT ARE THE STARS?

We know that the sun is 6,000°C (10,832°F) on its surface. This makes our Sun a yellow star. Red stars are about half this temperature. Though the red stars you see at night are very big, most of the red stars are in fact much smaller than our Sun. These small stars are not dying but are just normal stars that are too small to make much heat and light. This makes them red and very dull. You cannot see these small red stars at night because they are so faint. The sky at night is full of stars that are too faint to be seen. The blue stars are bright and twice as hot as our Sun.

Constellations

When you go outside at night the stars appear to make shapes and patterns. You may be able to see a kite or even a saucepan. Thousands of years ago the Greeks imagined stories called myths and illustrated them with the star patterns in the sky. We call these patterns constellations. There are eighty-eight constellations in the sky for you to find. Here are just two.

The red star at Orion's armpit is called Betelguese.

Sailors once used only the stars to find their way at night. This is called celestial navigation.

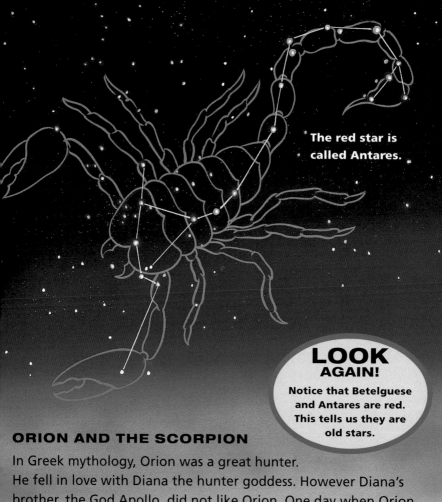

The red star is called Antares.

LOOK AGAIN!
Notice that Betelguese and Antares are red. This tells us they are old stars.

ORION AND THE SCORPION

In Greek mythology, Orion was a great hunter.
He fell in love with Diana the hunter goddess. However Diana's brother, the God Apollo, did not like Orion. One day when Orion was alone, Apollo took the great scorpion from the sky and set it on Orion. In fear, Orion jumped into the Mediterranean Sea and swam off to the horizon. Apollo went to find Diana and said, 'I bet you cannot hit that dot on the horizon with your bow and arrow.' Being a goddess, Diana did have the power to hit the distant speck. Days later Diana found Orion washed up on a beach. She was so sad that she placed Orion among the stars to be forever remembered. Orion now lies opposite the scorpion in the sky.

The Milky Way

Stretched right around the sky at night is the Milky Way. The early Greeks thought it was milk spilt on the sky. We now know that it is billions of very distant stars. Many of the stars are so far away you need a pair of binoculars or a telescope to see them.

MORE THAN JUST STARS

Away from the bright lights of a big city or town you can see the Milky Way as a band of stars across the sky. If you look along the band you can see dark patches where there seem to be no stars at all. These dark areas are where clouds of hydrogen gas are sitting in space. They are called nebulae. It is from nebulae that stars are born. More about this later.

Some of the stars you can see are points of light. Most of the stars are so far away they appear like a glowing mist in the sky.

WHY IS THERE A MILKY WAY?

The Milky Way is like a big, wide starry ribbon across the sky. You may think stars appear all over the sky, but they do not. We see many more stars along the Milky Way than elsewhere in the sky. Its biggest brightest part is near the constellation of the scorpion. At the end of the scorpion's tail you will see many stars. We see so many stars along the Milky Way because the stars and our Sun cluster in a big, flat group of stars in the shape of a saucer, called a galaxy. If we lived in a big ball of stars, we would see stars everywhere evenly across the sky.

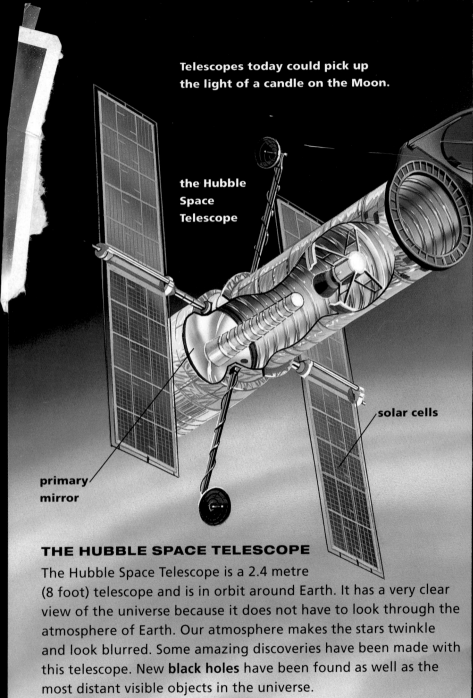

Telescopes today could pick up
the light of a candle on the Moon.

the Hubble
Space
Telescope

solar cells

primary
mirror

THE HUBBLE SPACE TELESCOPE

The Hubble Space Telescope is a 2.4 metre
(8 foot) telescope and is in orbit around Earth. It has a very clear
view of the universe because it does not have to look through the
atmosphere of Earth. Our atmosphere makes the stars twinkle
and look blurred. Some amazing discoveries have been made with
this telescope. New **black holes** have been found as well as the
most distant visible objects in the universe.

Telescopes

Telescopes make everything look closer and brighter. They are used by astronomers to explore the many different things in space.

MODERN TELESCOPES

Today there are many types of telescopes. There are telescopes that magnify the light coming from objects in space. These are called optical telescopes. There are some that pick up **radio waves** travelling from space. Some can even see **X-rays** coming from exploding stars. Very large optical telescopes are being built today. Nearly 400 years ago the first optical telescope was pointed at the sky by Galileo Galilei in Italy. This telescope was less than 25 millimetres (1 inch) across. Modern telescopes are 10 metres (33 feet) across!

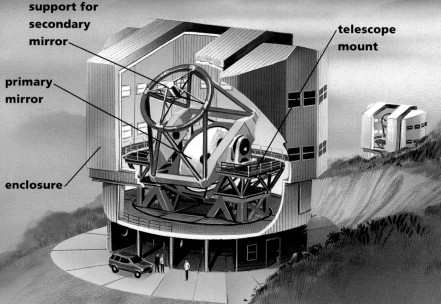

support for
secondary
mirror

telescope
mount

primary
mirror

enclosure

**One of the four 8 metre (26 foot) telescopes
in Chile, called The Very Large Telescope.**

systems

Astronomers have recently begun finding planets near other stars. They think that most of the stars will have planets. We don't know if there is any life on these planets.

DISTANT SOLAR SYSTEMS

For hundreds of years astronomers had wondered whether there were planets around stars other than our Sun. It seemed very unlikely that our solar system was the only one. However, finding a planet is very difficult. A planet is about 100 billion times fainter than a star. It is like trying to see an ant crawling around a headlight of a car when viewed from a distant 30 kilometres (19 miles) away. Because of this, astronomers cannot see planets near other stars. However, they can measure the way stars wobble as planets move about them. This tells astronomers many things about these new worlds.

LOOK AGAIN!

Which of these planets would you like to live on? Perhaps one of the ringed planets?

WHAT WOULD THEY BE LIKE?

Other solar systems may be very different to ours. They may have twenty or more planets, or maybe just one small planet. Astronomers may eventually find new worlds much bigger than Jupiter and with strange-looking living creatures. These distant aliens may look into their night sky and wonder what it may be like in other far-away solar systems. One day in the future we may talk with aliens from other worlds, but for now we can only imagine what these aliens would be like.

47

This is the great nebula in Orion. Hundreds of stars will eventually form from this cloud of gas and dust.

LIFE CYCLE OF STARS

Nebulae are made of hydrogen, helium and dust. Stars are hydrogen and helium pressed and held together by gravity. In the centre of a star, hydrogen explodes and creates the energy to make a star shine. Some stars are six times as big as our Sun. These stars can be 10 thousand times brighter and **blue hot**. When the hydrogen in the centre of a star runs out, the star dies. This will happen to the Sun in 5 billion years time. Stars a few times bigger than the Sun violently explode when they die. Not all of the star disintegrates. The central core of the star collapses down under the force of gravity to make a ball 20 kilometres (12 miles) across called a neutron star. If the original star is many times bigger than the Sun, the collapse does not stop. The star becomes a point with no size called a black hole. It has very strong gravity. Nothing can escape a black hole.

The birth of stars

Astronomers often talk about stars as though they are living things. They are not alive but astronomers say that stars have a birth, life and death. A star is born from a huge nebula. A star can die in an enormous explosion called a supernova.

Here a black hole is pulling gas off a giant star.

Galaxies

You and I are part of a very big universe. The universe is everything. When we look out into it we see that we belong to swirling groups of stars called a galaxy. There are many billions of galaxies in the universe.

We live on Earth, which is in the Solar System, which is in our Milky Way galaxy, which is one of many billions of galaxies in our universe.

Our Sun is one of 400 billion stars in our galaxy which is called the Milky Way galaxy.

Try counting all these stars and it would take you almost 13,000 years!

BIG BLUE SPIRALS

Galaxies often appear like big blue spirals—blue because the brightest stars in them are big, hot blue stars. The spirals are like big arms curling out from the centre of a galaxy. Along these arms new stars are being made in large nebulae. A galaxy compared to our Model Sun is 70 million kilometres (about 44 million miles) across (see page 11)! Compare this with the size of our imaginary solar system. Remember that Pluto would be only 490 metres (1,608 feet) from our Model Sun. Some galaxies are large balls of old stars. No new stars are being formed in these galaxies. Astronomers think these galaxies are spirals which have joined together. One day our Milky Way galaxy will collide with the Andromeda galaxy.

How did it all begin?

Astronomers think the universe began with a huge explosion, which they have called the Big Bang. If they are right, everything we see in the universe today came from the Big Bang.

Although scientists have calculated what the young universe was made up of, it is very difficult to imagine just what it looked like. No one was there to see it.

In the young universe there were no stars or galaxies. There was just a lot of hot gas and light.

AFTER THE BIG BANG

Astronomers think that the explosion happened about 14 billion years ago, but they are not sure. It is very difficult to work out exactly when the universe formed. But astronomers know that when it was young it was extremely hot, billions and billions of degrees Celsius. As the universe expanded away from the explosion, it became cooler. Hydrogen gas was made from the energy of the Big Bang. It took many hundreds of millions of years for the hydrogen to start making stars and galaxies. Today astronomers can look out into the universe and see all the galaxies rushing away from each other. The universe is still expanding all these years after the Big Bang. Scientists are not sure though what will happen in the future. Will the universe continue to get bigger, or will it slow down and pull itself together in a big crunch? Nobody knows.

The future

For thousands of years people have been wondering what is out in space. Once upon a time, they thought it was the home of gods—a place too special and mysterious for people to visit. Today, with the help of telescopes and spacecraft, we can explore space and see what it is like.

REACHING OUT INTO SPACE

We know there are many stars and planets in the universe, just like in our solar system. For now, the stars are too far away for our spacecraft to visit. It would take hundreds of thousands of years to make the journey. The planets in our solar system are much closer. We know what they look like from the pictures sent to us by spacecraft.

LIVING ON MARS

So far no one has ever travelled to a planet in a spacecraft, though one day soon people will do so. Mars will be the first. Maybe ten years from now astronauts will be flying to the 'red planet'. It will take them six months to get there. They will have to take lots of food and water for the journey. When they arrive they will explore Mars wearing spacesuits that supply them with air and water. These explorers will also make special homes to live in. How wonderful it will be for them to see a Martian sky and experience a Martian day. They will see a sunset and may even eat the first fruit grown from the Martian soil. Would you like to be the first? I know I would.

LOOK AGAIN!

The sand on the side of the domes has slowly gathered there after many dust storms.

Driving to a star

Drive to the stars in a car? I do not think so. It is a very long way to go!

OUR SPECIAL SPACE CAR

If you could drive through space in a car that travels at 100 kilometres (60 miles) per hour you may think that after one day you had gone a long way. However, you would still be very close to home compared to the distance to a star. In our special space car it would take you 5 months to reach the Moon. The Sun would be close after 170 years but then you would have to wait 45 million years to arrive at Alpha Centauri, the nearest star to us in the night sky. If people are ever to visit the stars we will need a spaceship much faster than our car.

In the distant future people will visit the stars. They will explore planets around other stars and maybe even meet aliens and show them pictures of our distant planet Earth.

See for yourself...

- Go outside on a clear night an hour after sunset and look at the stars. First, try and see the different colours in the stars. Most will be white and blue, but a few will be red.

- Keep looking up and you may see what appears to be stars moving slowly across the sky. These are satellites that are orbiting a few hundred kilometres above you.

- Now look for flashes of light across the sky. These are meteors entering the atmosphere and burning up. It may take 5 minutes or maybe half an hour, but if you are patient you will see one.

- You may have noticed that the sky is moving. To see this easily, find a star that is near a building. Stand very still and watch. You will see the star appears to be moving very, very slowly. This is because Earth you are standing on is spinning.

GLOSSARY

astronaut Someone trained to travel to space in a spacecraft. Many astronauts are also scientists who carry out experiments.

atmosphere A layer of gas surrounding a planet, moon or star held on by gravity.

atoms Very small particles that combine together to make everything in the universe. About 5 million atoms could fit side by side across 1 millimetre ($\frac{1}{25}$ inch). There are over 100 different types of atoms.

black hole A place in space where the gravity is so strong that no radiation can escape and where anything approaching it will disappear.

blue hot Anything over 10 thousand degrees Celsius. It will glow with a blue light.

crater A hole in the ground caused by the collision of a rock from space.

day The 24 hour period of time from one midnight to the next.

dust Very fine pieces of rocky material.

eroded Worn away by the movement of air and water.

erupting Bursting or exploding from the surface of something such as a planet, star, moon, etc.

galaxy A group of between a million to about a million million stars held together by gravity. Each one can have a different shape. Most are spiral, some are like a big ball, and a few look quite odd.

gas A substance like air made up of freely moving **atoms.**

gravity Everything attracts everything else with the force of gravity. Things fall towards Earth because of gravity.

helium The second-lightest **atom.** Helium gas is sometimes used to fill balloons which will then be lighter than air and float.

hydrogen The lightest **atom.**

Kuiper object Icy objects just past the orbit of Neptune. They may vary in size from no bigger than a grain of sand to the size of Pluto.

GLOSSARY

meteor A rock that enters Earth's atmosphere and burns up.

meteorite A rock that enters Earth's atmosphere and hits the ground.

nebula (NEB-yoo-lah) An enormous cloud of hydrogen, helium and dust out in space. For more than one we say nebulae (NEB-yoo-lie).

neutron star An object about 20 kilometres (12 miles) across that is the collapsed remains of a massive star.

orbit (noun) The path objects follow when circling around another object. For example, the path the planets take when circling around the Sun.

orbit (verb) To circle around another object.

radio waves Radiation that is like light but a million times weaker. Many objects in space are observed to give out radio waves. These can be observed with radio telescopes.

satellite An object that orbits a planet. Many thousands of satellites have been made that orbit Earth. The moon is a natural satellite of Earth.

solar wind A stream of small particles that race away from the Sun in all directions with a speed of about 400 kilometres (250 miles) every second.

supernova The explosion of a massive star. The explosion can make as much light as 100 billion stars.

universe Everything that can be seen and may be able to be seen and the space they occupy.

X-rays Radiation like light but a hundred thousand times more energetic. Many objects in space are observed to give out X-rays. These can be observed with X-ray telescopes.

year The length of time it takes Earth to orbit the Sun.

FIND OUT MORE ABOUT SPACE

BOOKS

Bond, Peter, *Guide to Space,* Dorling Kindersley, London, 1999.

Dyer, Alan, *Space,* Reader's Digest, Sydney, 1999.

Furniss, Tim, *Astronomy Factfinder,* Mustard, Bath, England, 1999.

Graham, Ian, *Space,* Lorenz Books, London, 1999.

WEBSITES

Hubble Heritage Project
http://heritage.stsci.edu/public/gallery/galindex.html

Space Science Mission
http://www.hg.nasa.gov/office/oss/missions/index/htm

Welcome to the Planets
http://pds.jpl.nasa.gov/planets/

INDEX

INDEX

INDEX

FREE

INVESTIGATE

POSTER!

Collect 6 of the gold **INVESTIGATE** stickers

(you will find one on the stickers' page in each book).

**Send all 6 stickers on a sheet of paper
along with your name and address to:**

Investigate Series Poster
Whitecap Books
351 Lynn Avenue
North Vancouver
British Columbia
V7J 2C4

and we'll send you your free **INVESTIGATE series poster.**

Please allow 21 days for delivery.